SPIRITUAL
PERSPECTIVES
— *on* —
DEATH
& DYING

Bernice H. Hill, Ph.D.

Luminous Moon Press
Boulder, CO

Cover photo "Starry night sky and Milky Way over
Jackson Lake and Tetons" copyright Royce Baird.
Cover and interior layout and design by
Carolyn Oakley, Luminous Moon Design.

First Edition
First Printing: September 2015

Publication Data
Bernice Hill
Spiritual Perspectives on Death and Dying

ISBN-13: 978-0-9968600-0-0
Ontology – Death and Dying – New Consciousness
Spirituality – Jungian Psychology

Printed and bound in the United States of America

ACKNOWLEDGEMENTS

Over the years, many people have contributed to this "gathering" of thoughts and reflections. In particular, I would like to thank Ann Allegre, Stephanie Bendel, Celia Coates, Paul and Mimi Hansen, Jeffrey Kiehl, Jane Kircher, Donna Mitchell-Moniak, and Joy Om. I would like to give a special note of appreciation to Carolyn Oakley for her preparation of the material for publication.

CONTENTS

*"A man should be able to say he has done his best to form a
conception of life after death or to create some image of it –
Not to have done so is a vital loss."*

Carl Jung
Memories, Dreams and Reflections

Introduction

THE GATHERING CLOUDS

 It was a watershed moment. My heart beat faster when I saw where the letter had come from—my doctor. Then, in professional language, the message, simple and direct: *Your recent mammogram showed several irregularities. Please call to schedule a follow-up appointment.*

A geographical watershed is a high point of land—all rivers become divided. On one side, they may flow east and on the other, west. Psychologically, it is an awakening. Consciousness suddenly finds itself in a whole new reality, flowing in a different direction.

These writings stem from that moment. At age 79, I was shocked by the diagnosis of invasive breast cancer that followed. I could no longer pretend I was aging gracefully. Suddenly, I was no longer immortal.

The time had come to face this profoundly mysterious and threatening future: a threshold faced by all. Over the years I had witnessed others going through this doorway; heard many stories of their passages, but now it was my turn. This was different. Real and immediate!

My approach was typical for me; I wanted an overview. Not so much of the progress of breast cancer, but the more important wake-up call of facing death. I would gather everything I could find on the subject —the full range of ideas, theories, philosophical approaches, personal stories and courageous antidotes.

The following chapters trace that endeavor, and I have come to realize that it was a task that had been waiting for me for years.

Chapter 1

CARL JUNG

In the spring of 1993, I drove to the house of a patient of mine who was very ill with bowel cancer. The quiet, tidy green squares of suburban lawn curved around the corner where he lived. The sun glowed through the new green leaves and I wondered what it must feel like to be dying, when the warm earth was just coming back.

Betty answered the door and led us down the hall. Bob was talking to the Hospice nurse, so I mustered those things one says to an anxious wife. Memories of the angry marital sessions between them floated through my mind. The nurse left.

Bob was weary and a bad color. I said I would go, but he motioned for me to sit down. With great effort, he hoisted himself to his feet and headed for the bathroom. Shortly thereafter, there was a cry. Betty rushed to him, calling for my help. The weakened man drooped on the toilet, breathing hard. The gray-green color of his face deepened. Betty, pale as slate, was trying to hold him.

The man was heavy on our arms. With my face a few inches from his head, I could see the beads of sweat on his forehead and smell the stale odors of bedclothes and tired body. Fear gripped Betty.

"Talk to him," I said. This angry woman, who rarely had anything positive to say, started murmuring, "I love you, Bob. You have been a fine husband and a wonderful father. Things will be all right!" She stroked the damp, bald, head.

Bob gave one long labored sigh and his body slumped. In awkward ways, we just held him, saying nothing. Later, we laid the body on the floor, covered it and called for help. As I contemplated this death, I remembered how often Betty had said she was terrified that Bob would die in their bed in the middle of the night and then she would be alone! In bed with Death! This thought haunted her and yet, here we were together with something rather simple.

It was an amazing day for me, for that afternoon I had interviews with three committees for acceptance into a rigorous national training program to become a Jungian analyst. As would be expected for those interested in the work of C. G. Jung, their first question was "Did you

have any dream last night before these interviews?"
I swallowed hard when I remembered what
it was:

I am in the backyard of my house. There is a stone
wall there about four feet high. On it is inscribed:

"Beneath the wide and starry sky,
Lay me down and let me die,
Home is the sailor, home from the sea.
And the hunter home from the hills." [1]

To the right of this wall stood Christ, looking very
weary and frustrated with me!

Of course, the committee wanted to know what
I made of this. Why the theme of death and why was
Christ frustrated with me? I was totally surprised by
the whole turn of events. I had been brought up in a
Christian home; my Protestant parents were respectful
of those beliefs. Why was it important for me to have a
clearer understanding of death as the natural order of
things?

In retrospect, my entry into the Jungian training
program was a tremendous opportunity to address these
personal issues, for Carl Jung was fascinated by death.

I was drawn to the work of Carl Jung because of his strong belief that life was meaningful. Of all those who have set themselves the task of exploring the human psyche, Jung stands out as a man with strong faith that there was fundamental purpose in the soul's journey.

Nowhere was this more evident than in his approach to death. The reality of death in everyone's life sets the stage for basic questions. Are we moved, over the course of life, toward some deeply sensed goal? Or, are we just driven by ego, physical and sexual needs? If it is useful for the spiritual person to see death as a goal, then aging and approaching death should be the focus, in the second half of life, for meditative reflection.

Jung's great gift was to show that within each of us is a process whereby we can open to and dialogue with the vast, rich storehouse of the unconscious. Here are the ancient archetypes of death and rebirth found in cultures around the earth and across time.

Communing with the symbols and visions that arise from the unconscious, we are given insights about our shortcomings and their role in the panorama of human dilemmas. Here is where we can find balance and, unexpectedly, profound guidance. Here is the dialogue that nudges us toward maturity.

Jung writes that thoughts of death pile up in an older person. There are so many unknowns around "when" and "how." There is the natural fear of the process of dying, and the possibility of pain and suffering. The fears of becoming vulnerable, losing control, and the indignities of death are part of it. There is also the sorrow of all the separations involved: from loved ones, friends, meaningful identities, and familiar surroundings. For some, there may be anxieties from the teachings about heaven and hell or from a lack of any sustaining beliefs. And underlying it all, is the fear that the self will cease to exist.

There are vicissitudes to be encountered. Jung would say that these challenges take on a larger meaning, if we are willing to face them and not take the easy way out of denial. We have, in the process of dying, a basic need to connect to something greater within. Jung also wrote that the more he looked into it, the more he was astonished to see how little *"ado"* the unconscious psyche actually makes about death. The unconscious believes in life after death and assumes that *it* has the *real* story and conscious life is *"the illusion."*

Marie Louis Von Franz, a protégé of Jung, wrote a book called *Dreams and Death*. She collected many dreams of people of all ages just before they died. These dreams reflected Jung's observation. Here is one of a forty year-old man, who had been told he did not have long to live.

> *There is a green, half-high, not-yet-ripe wheat field.*
> *A herd of cattle had broken in and trampled it down.*
> *Then a voice called out, "everything seems to be*
> *destroyed, but from the roots under the earth the*
> *wheat will grow again."*

Von Franz reported that the man, a client, did not believe the encouraging message of dream and died shortly afterward, not having reconciled himself to his early death.

Another dream Von Franz described was of a young woman who, although unconscious most of the time, awoke briefly just before she died to report the following:

> *I am standing beside my bed in the hospital room.*
> *Sunshine flows in through the window. The doctor is*
> *there and says, "Well, Miss X, you are unexpectedly*
> *completely cured. You may get dressed and leave the*
> *hospital." At that moment I turn around and see,*
> *lying in the bed, my own dead body.*

Here, the unconscious considered death to be "the cure," for now it was able to leave a body totally taken over by cancer. It was free to go on.

Von Franz did say that some dying people had oppressive "passage" dreams. Death for them was a journey of deep fear of the darkness, of losing consciousness and ego identity. Von Franz compared these dreams to the old alchemical texts, where death and rebirth applied not only to the end of life, but to all major psychic crises and transformative experiences.

Von Franz also noted their similarity to myths of death found in ancient cultures. For example, early Egyptian stories described how dying souls followed the path of the sun descending into the night of the underworld. There, they underwent "the night sea journey," where they had to overcome various obstructions before they would rise again in the east.

In Jungian thought, the degree of darkness encountered in dying relates to how well a person has developed a relationship to the Self. Jung believed that the Self is the Center, the source and ultimate foundation of our psychic being. It is our Essence and it generates the symbols and visions that lead to deeper wisdom. Over a lifetime, we gradually realize that those things that move us deeply or arise with the profound feeling that "this is right," come from the Self. And sometimes, the presence in dreams of the Christ figure represents the Self.

Von Franz's work confirmed that when the dreams occurring just before death were oppressive, there often had been little acknowledgement during the lifetime of the reality of the Self. Such dreamers would then encounter it as an ominous presence, perhaps like a dark cloud. The Self can confront us; but, if with patience, we allow the symbolism to unfold, the meaning becomes clear.

This was a dream of an elderly woman on the day she died:

I see a candle lit on the windowsill of the hospital room. The candle suddenly goes out. I am very afraid. The darkness envelops me. But suddenly, the candle lights again on the other side of the window.

Here was direct information from the Self on the passage of death. For this woman, the fear and depression were brief and she died in peace.

Von Franz found that images of light and numinosity (the sacred) appeared more often than any other, in the dream material she had gathered. She connected this to Jung's thinking that within our material body lay the higher frequencies of super-luminous light. This light would be the last thing seen before one's psyche faded. Here was a dream of a Protestant clergyman, a few days before his death:

I see the clock on the mantelpiece; the hands have been moving, but now they stop. As they stop, a window opens behind the mantelpiece clock and a bright light shines through. The opening widens into a door and the light becomes a brilliant path. I walk out on the path of light and disappear.

Jung was one of the few Western psychologists to take life after death seriously. He always had an interest in the occult and subtle energies. In the *Red Book,* he writes of his dialogues with Death. He, himself, had three near-death experiences and, reportedly, also had numerous private conversations with associates on reincarnation. (see Bibliography: *Row of Tombs: Jung and Reincarnation* by Sabine Lucas)

Jung often remarked that he felt his life was like a rhizome: an underground root system which grows horizontally and adds new shoots each year. The part that appears above ground lasts only one summer (one lifetime), but then continues underneath, to sprout a new plant the following spring.

A few days before Jung's death he had a dream of wholeness and completion, which ended with the images of—*a quadrangle of trees whose roots reached around the earth and enveloped it. Among the roots, golden threads were glittering.*

This was the dream of a man who had finished what he had come to do and had given the gift he was meant to give.

NOTES

1. This half-remembered poem is a version of Robert Louise Stephenson's "Requiem."

Chapter 2

STANISLAV GROF

The natural successor to Jung and his exploration of our deep psyche is Stanislav Grof, one of the original researchers of LSD. In 1963, Grof was involved in designing a project for the terminally ill at the Spring Grove Hospital in Baltimore.[1]

The Spring Grove program that Grof developed was a volunteer project that ran for seven years. Over 100 people, dying of cancer, participated. After extensive preparation, individuals were given dosages of LSD, specific to their condition, and encouraged to follow their inner experience. The sessions usually lasted ten to twelve hours; profound music was played much of the time. Supportive therapy followed each session so that all experiences could be integrated.

The outcome for two-thirds of the group was a significant reduction in depression and anxiety about death. The lowering of fear led to a lessening of pain and need for medication. The majority of patients reported improvements in mood and rapport with family and friends.

When research with psychedelics was curtailed, Grof and his wife, Christine, developed a process they called Holotropic Breathwork™. This intervention used the accelerated breathing found in ancient Hindu meditative practices. The Grofs interwove the enhanced breathing with evocative music and minimal bodywork. They found that similar non-ordinary states of consciousness occur with Holotropic Breathwork™ as with psychedelics.

Over the years, thousands of people from all walks of life and with many different physical and emotional conditions, have participated in these sessions.

It is instructive to look more closely at the increasingly deeper levels of the psyche revealed by Grof's work. As one enters the therapeutic process (using either psychedelics or Holotropic Breathwork™) one first finds oneself exploring the personal unconscious. Here, early traumas, both physical and emotional, arise and can be relived. As one goes deeper, one can even encounter the time in the womb and the subsequent birthing process. These memories are very intense and remembered in great detail. They feel life threatening;

for the fetus to leave the safety of the uterus is a type of death experience.

Grof found there were four stages of a person's birthing process that can arise. The first was the pre-birth state of security, and union with the mother. At this stage, there was a sense of peace and tranquility where all needs were instantly met. Stage two occurred as the chemical composition of the uterus changed and the muscle contractions began. Now, the fetus experienced a sense of foreboding, a darkening of the perceptual field, and a fear of being imprisoned. With its motion curtailed, there were intense feelings of helplessness, a "dark night of the soul." The third stage occurred with passage down the birth canal. Here, the fetus was subjected to crushing pressures and suffocation. Memories of immense struggle characterized this passage. The fourth stage was surrender and release into a new world, a sense of being liberated from the compression, of expanding into brilliant light. The baby felt the relief of finding a new way to breathe; and after being washed and warmed, was filled with a blissful sense of ease.

There were other gifts in these altered state journeys that would arrive after the birthing experience. Participants recalled their past lives and accessed racial and ancestral memories. Deities, spirits and archetypal figures were encountered. As consciousness expanded, accurate information was gained on animals, plants, inorganic matter and processes, and mythic realms. Details of historical periods and issues became known; although there was no way the participant had this information prior to the experience.

In the deepest transpersonal states, participants opened to insights long described in the ancient spiritual traditions. They would move into the Primary Clear Light or Universal Mind and places of sublime peace and equanimity. It became clear that, under those expanded states, humans have access to all the cosmic levels. Indeed, we are composed of the same basic cosmic creative principle that moves through the Universe. What the mystics of all ages have claimed has now been repeatedly confirmed by Grof's work.

Many of the terminally ill who went through the journeys with psychedelics also relived the deep, experiential journey of birth. They came to realize that birth and death were mirror images of each other and that they had been through these turbulent transitions before. Grof suggested that the type of birth the person had experienced might influence the intensity of their fears about death.

In his book *The Ultimate Journey*, Grof presents detailed accounts of the LSD experience of a number of dying patients in the Spring Grove program. A full reading of the material is necessary to understand the complexity and intensity of this experimental psychotherapy. Each participant, with their own unique background and set of conditions, underwent a wide variety of intense physical sensations and emotional feelings. They all saw the patterns and conflicts of their life trajectories. However, the confrontation with death inherent in the process led to a profound healing and expansion of awareness. Here are a few, brief descriptions of their journeys:

Ted, a 26 year-old African American, married with three children and dying of colon cancer, relived earlier deaths in many threatening situations, such as war, epidemics, and accidents. Astonished, he saw the eternal cycles of life and death unfolding before his eyes. No one in these situations really died. Nothing was really destroyed. All experienced a transition to a different kind of existence. Ted came to appreciate that everything was in eternal flux and transformation.

Joan was a 40 year-old housewife, mother of four children with advanced stomach cancer who, after several surgeries, underwent three LSD sessions before her death. She reported that the most important aspect of the sessions was her understanding of "the big picture." She said she saw the unfolding of the cosmic design in all its infinite nuances. Each individual represented a thread in the beautiful warp of life and was playing a specific role. All these roles were equally necessary for the central core of the universe; none of them was more important than others. After death, the life energy underwent a transformation and the roles were recast.

Catherine was a 60 year-old businesswoman, with breast cancer that had metastasized to the liver. During her sessions she re-experienced many painful times from her childhood. As one session developed, she found herself fighting the sucking force of the birthing vortex. She felt a shattering of her skull; then she was a tiny baby choking on something from the birth canal. This led gradually to a shimmering vision of a giant wheel, with images of all the world's religions inscribed on the rim. These images fused into one and she was flooded with sensations of warmth and light: the Divine within, transcending all forms and boundaries.

After fifty years of facilitating psychedelic and Holotropic Breathwork™ processes with thousands of participants around the world, Grof has documented the deep transpersonal realms that exist within us. He writes:

"I have seen many atheists, materialists, skeptics, Marxists and positive scientists reach this point and experience a radical change in their world view. The spirituality that opens up in this context has nothing to do with organized religion—it is mystical, universal, non-denominational and all encompassing."
– The Ultimate Journey, pg. 311

For the terminally ill, these inner encounters with death and rebirth, taught them the wisdom of surrender. It was through their acceptance of the dying process and "letting go" that all things began to flow into the much deeper and wider perspective. They gained faith in their passage ahead.

* * * * *

The great Buddhist teacher, Sogyal Rinpoche, has written that for all its technological achievements, modern Western society has no real understanding of death, of what happens in death or what happens after death.

Jung and Grof's efforts in modern consciousness research have given us a more comprehensive map of our inner reality. Their explorations have softened our overly materialistic view of who and what we are. They have provided us with a psychological bridge to the great mystical traditions on death that have come to us from the East.

The many spiritual texts from the Orient have great variation in their terms and definitions. In the next chapters, I look briefly at only three of the major Oriental perspectives on the subject. The first is the Hindu. It emerged from the mists of time in approximately 4000 BCE. In its Vedic texts (written around 1500 BCE) man is described as living in relationship to the Divine and in a world to which he belongs. The next perspective I have chosen is Tibetan Buddhism, which arose around the 6th century AD. The third perspective comes from the esoteric teachings of Djwal Khul. It is called the Ageless Wisdom tradition and is found in the extensive writings of Alice Bailey.

* * * * *

NOTES

1. While psychedelic research has been curtailed for over forty years, it is now slowly returning and showing marked results with certain populations. Programs for the terminally ill have been conducted at Harvard's Medical School and UCLA's Medical Center in Los Angeles.

Chapter 3

HINDU PERSPECTIVE

The sun filtered down through the sea pines, catching their rough bark and lighting the sandy path. I was meditating by a quiet koi pond in the garden of the Hindu center in Encinitas, California. The large, beautiful, multi-colored fish swam languidly, their bright red and yellow sides showing each time they turned. The air was gentle, quiet and fragrant with all the surrounding flowers. The only sound was the distant swish of the Pacific lapping the early morning shore.

As I sat there, I spied a small round pebble at my feet and thought, "I should take this home in memory of such a lovely moment in my life." "No," said a counter voice in my head. "Each element here belongs in *this* place. What you need to do is re-read *Autobiography of a Yogi* by the Hindu sage Paramahansa Yogananda."

On my return to Colorado I did just that and wondered how I could learn more about the Kriya yoga practice, which was Yogananda's great gift for our Western mind. Kriya yoga activates energies that move along the spine. This practice opens the spiritual eye (thought to be located between the physical eyes) and when enlivened, expands intuition and leads to higher subtle realms.

That week there arrived a notice in the mail that The Caritas Spiritual Center (a mile from my front door) was sponsoring a Swamiji (Hindu teacher). His name was Yogacharya Dharmananda, and he was teaching Kriya yoga and giving courses on Hindu philosophy. He also was working with the staff of a number of local hospitals on issues of death and dying.

* * * * *

As noted earlier, the Hindu view of death and dying arises from the wisdom of Vedanta (the Vedas), the teachings of countless spiritual teachers (rishis) of India. In Vedanta understanding of reality, the whole Universe is intelligent, permeated with consciousness and in continuous evolution. As humans, we are connected to this infinite consciousness in our own long journey of transformation and creativity.

Here are a few passages from the texts:

Arjuna was afraid to die, but Krishna helped him.
– Bhagavad Gita

Attachment to bodily residence, springing up of its own nature, is present in slight degree even in great saints.
– Patanjali

...Just as a long, caged bird hesitates to leave its accustomed home when the door is opened.
– Paramahansa Yogananda

To the Hindus, dying is a process that allows us to profoundly experience the force of evolution. For in dying, we are confronted with all our attachments and the realization that they must be released. This includes our identification with the body.

Death occurs when the original karmic impulse[2] for a life has no more to teach. To the Hindu, moving into the "afterlife" does not mean a change of location, but a change in the state of awareness. Death is just one aspect of the soul's long journey to Spirit. Through reincarnation[2], the soul acquires finer and finer vibrations until it reaches the *stillness* of pure Awareness.

Vedanta states that all humans are under the compelling influence of three *gunas* or motivating energies of Nature. They are: *tamas* (ignorance or inertia), *ragas* (activity or struggle) and *sattva* (wisdom.) We have to be in a physical body to work with these forces. We need to experience our particular blend of these energies and become aware of their power within us.

Each experience of the gunas produces a seed, called a *samskara*.[2] These samskaras become like imprints on a disc in our psyche; they urge us to certain repeated actions. For spiritual growth, these habitual patterns need to be recognized and burned away. This would apply to our compulsions and unconscious impulses. We can find them in the story lines that reverberate in our heads.

Over our lifetime, we come to recognize those people who have accomplished the difficult work of personal and spiritual growth. We see them as "good people'" and occasionally "saintly people" and, even more rarely, "angelic people." They give us evidence that there has been a perceptual shift which has created a different inner environment, a new sense of self. Such shifts affect their outlook on life and the after–death journey.

Hindus consider that when we are born the soul enters three levels of the human constitution:

- Physical – five senses, basic functions of brain and body
- Astral – the *energetic* blueprint of our body, invisible, but luminous
- Causal – the original idea or thought forms that underlie our astral and physical bodies

Each of these levels has its own vibrational frequency and instruments of perception. Each follows its own particular rules. There is a progression in vibrational frequency from gross (physical) to fine (causal).

Yogananda writes that for us to understand the dying process we need to know that our consciousness is actually "locked" in these three rooms, one inside of the other (physical, astral and causal). It requires the unlocking of all three doors to ultimately return us to Source. This "return" is a foundational idea of the three Eastern perspectives considered here, and is thought to be the natural archetypal path of our Spirit.

When an ordinary man dies, the soul withdraws life from the first room (the physical), but still remains locked in the astral and causal bodies. Within the many levels of the astral realm he will find himself at a frequency level that corresponds to the maturity he obtained in physical life. Those souls who have made spiritual advancement while incarnated will be on a higher astral level. Having worked more consciously with their innate gunas, some may even move to the causal plane. These assignments of "location" follow the rule that you only "see" what you vibrate to. It is the quality and focus of your attention that actually shifts in maturation.

For most people, death will be an experience of deep sleep, interspersed with certain astral visions of positive or negative content, depending on the life led. Eventually, the soul "revives to the ceaseless activity of desire" and becoming aware of its predominant desires, reincarnates on the physical plane.

Deepak Chopra, raised in both the Christian and Hindu traditions, expands the description.[1] He writes that as we die and the gross senses fade, the subtle senses sharpen. We enter the astral field where we immediately feel lighter, sensing a new freedom from all physical limitations. Our astral body is a mirror of our physical body. We still retain a sense of "I" and the feeling of moving on to another plane of existence.

We may experience the "heaven" or "hell" which reflects our own beliefs and continuing projections. For example, while Christians may find themselves in a place of redemption, peopled with figures from that worldview, those of other faiths will find the images that fit their particular beliefs. Vedic tradition says the afterlife will give us what we are expecting.

Chopra shapes his descriptions of death in the larger picture of continuity. He notes the astral realm is not unknown to us. We often visit it in our sleep. Those who are clairvoyant, telepathic or engage in "out of body" travel are aware of it. Altered states open us to the entities, guides and ghosts that can inhabit the astral realms.

With his Hindu background, Chopra is comfortable with reincarnation. He notes that the rishis saw the Universe as constantly recreating itself. It would not make sense if human consciousness was the only aspect not involved in that. Consciousness is too special a quality to be lost. The soul is a process which, surviving death, is released from the confines of the physical body. Now with greater awareness beyond time and space, it can review the life just lived and see more clearly the operation of the law of cause and effect. It will witness the errors and rewards, sense the innate need for meaning and responsibility.

Chopra comments that, if while living, we had developed self-awareness, intention, and discrimination, a new freedom and opportunity opens up for us. After death, there is a sense of a flowing, mysterious state of consciousness that actually is profoundly creative. Thoughts can be used to instantly create images. We can make choices and we can influence situations. He notes, that even the process of reincarnation can be enhanced by greater choice—of the best learning environment for us to move into the next life.

The ancient Vedic texts report that when yogis die, they also benefit from the spiritual work done during their lifetime. They have trained themselves, through years of meditation, to "open the spiritual eye." This eye, located between the two physical eyes, is inwardly sensed. When opened, one's visual spherical field expands bringing experiences of great light and joy. For this reason, Hindus call it "the bindi" and mark their foreheads with red ochre. Symbolically, the bindi represents the honor to be dedicated to the concealed wisdom within, and is thought to help strengthen the energy needed to concentrate on that area of the forehead.

In opening the visual field of the third eye, yogis can direct their attention sequentially through four concentric tubes of energy that make up the flowing life force within the spine. Three of these tubes are *astral* in nature, but the innermost tube is *causal.*

As they die, the yogis are able to take their life energy through the outer golden rings of the astral realm. (Those who have "near death experiences" and report moving through a tunnel to a beautiful light are likely experiencing this phenomenon.) Passing through the next doorway, the yogis enter the blue region of the spiritual eye, known as the causal realm. With further training, the yogis see a tiny silvery white star, and moving through this, go beyond the causal realm to ascend into Brahman (Infinite Spirit).

> *"He attains the Supreme effulgent Lord, O Arjuna, whose mind stabilized by yoga, is immovably fixed on the thought of Him. At the time of death the yogi reaches the Supreme Effulgent Lord if, with the love and power of yoga, he fully penetrates his life force between the eyebrows (the seat of the spiritual eye), and if he fixes his mind unwaveringly on the Being who, beyond all delusions of darkness, shines like the sun — The One whose form is unimaginable, subtler than the finest atom, the Supporter of all, the Great Ruler, eternal and omniscient."*
>
> – God Talks to Arjuna: The Bhagavad Gita, v111: 8-10

While most of us in the Western world are not awake to these specific processes, it is comforting to know that they are possible. Christian visions and prayers likely carry our own potential for these experiences.

Paramahansa Yogananda made a great effort to bring to us the Eastern spiritual teachings with which he was raised. A skilled writer, he provided a bridge between Eastern and Western spiritual traditions. Particularly important was his work: *The Second Coming of Christ: The Resurrection of the Christ Within You.* Here, he interwove *every passage* in the New Testament with Vedic thought.

I wanted to explore these writings further to see, in particular, how he considered the death of Lazarus, as well as Jesus' crucifixion and resurrection. Here are the terms that Yogananda used:

God: the Creator, Divine Supporter of All: boundless, beyond any vibration of form.

Cosmic Consciousness: the potential Absolute; arises in samadhi-meditation states of oneness with God, both within and beyond vibratory creation.

Christ Consciousness: also referred to as Cosmic Christ and Christ Intelligence, the projected consciousness of God immanent in all manifest creation.

Holy Ghost: is the sacred Intelligent Vibration from God that structures and sustains all of Creation. Referenced in Vedic tradition as the continual resonant AUM (Om) vibration and in the West as Amen. Merging with the AUM vibration, yogis enter the spiritual eye.

Resurrection of Lazarus

The raising of Lazarus is an extraordinary event and is explored by Yogananda in some detail. He writes that it is one of the most instructive teachings of Jesus. It reinforces both Christian beliefs in the afterlife, as well as the Hindu perspective of what the soul encounters during the dying process.

> *"Now a certain man was sick, named Lazarus, of Bethany, the town of Mary and her sister Martha...Therefore his sisters sent unto Jesus, saying 'Lord, behold, he whom thou lovest is sick'."*
> – John 12:3

Jesus, who was miles away in Jordan, said to his disciples, *"Our friend Lazarus sleepeth; but I go that I may wake him out of sleep."* To this, the disciples replied, *"Lord, if he sleep, he shall do well."* They were, of course, thinking in ordinary terms.

Jesus, however, tarried; *"He abode two days still in the same place where he was."* Yogananda notes that Jesus allowed Lazarus's karma to take its destined course. This delay was intentional, for it set up the situation that would demonstrate Jesus's mastery over the divine laws of the physical and karmic processes.

When they did arrive in Bethany, Martha, distraught over the death of her brother, said to Jesus, *"Lord, if thou hadst been here, my brother would not have died."*

Jesus responds with, *"I am the resurrection...he that believeth in me..."* Writing in depth about this response, Yogananda suggests that these remarks of Jesus to Martha point to the reality that within us there are many higher levels of consciousness, ultimately available.

Jesus said, *"Take away the stone." Martha, the sister of him that was dead, saith unto him,"Lord, by this time he stinketh for he hath been dead four days."*

And Jesus lifted up his eyes and said, *"Father, I thank Thee that Thou has heard me. And I know that Thou hearest me always: but because of the people, which stand by, I say it, that they may believe that Thou hast sent me."*
– John 11:41-42

Yogananda translates this prayer in his Hindu way as,

"Over-conscious, ever-wise Father, infinite Cosmic Consciousness, I thank Thee that Thou has vibrated Thine absolute power in the Christ Consciousness in me...I know with certainty and intuition that Thou dost always vibrate Thine omnipotence of Cosmic Consciousness in response to the vibrating divine wishes in my Christ Intelligence."
– The Second Coming of Christ, pg. 1168

The New Testament continues with:

"And when he thus had spoken, he cried with a loud voice, 'Lazarus, come forth.' And he that was dead came forth, bound hand and foot with grave clothes: his face bound about with a napkin. Jesus saith unto them, 'Loose him, and let him go'."
– John 11: 43-44

Yogananda describes the exceptional power of Jesus in this event. He had, at first, to make contact with Lazarus in the astral world. Then, by projecting his own consciousness into the dead body, Jesus would take onto himself the force of the specific karma that had compelled Lazarus' soul to leave. Once this was absorbed and neutralized, Jesus would command the

Cosmic Energy to restore the viability of the cells with all their astral and causal capacities for life. Then, he would invite the soul of Lazarus to re-inhabit the body, which now had regained all the powers of knowledge, action, mind and energy that had been released in the dying process.

Yogananda writes that this healing of Lazarus was done not only out of compassion for Mary and Martha, but to demonstrate that latent within every soul is the potential power to attain higher levels of effective consciousness. It exists and can be accessed.

The Crucifixion and Resurrection

Yogananda writes in great depth of all the events leading up to the crucifixion of Jesus. He does this not to detract in any way from the profound impact of the Crucifixion as expressed in the New Testament. He does it only to share his Hindu understanding of what happened. He sees each action and statement in terms of the purpose that Jesus came to fulfill. This purpose fully aligns with the Hindu thought:

> *"The Self is never born, nor does it ever perish; nor having come into existence will it again cease to be. It is birth-less, eternal, changeless, ever-the-same (unaffected by the usual processes associated*

with time). It is not slain when the body is killed."
– The Second Coming of Christ, pg. 1469

Yogananda explores Jesus's experience on the cross by focusing on Jesus's comments during the dying process. The human cry, *"My God, my God, why hast Thou forsaken me?"* does not detract from the greatness of Jesus, but connects us to him and strengthens the reality of the pain of the cruel way he was put to death. Without that event, we might not truly understand how the man (and mankind) was both human and divine.

Yoganada writes:

It would be easy for an immortal god wearing a body but unaffected by it, to play out a part of sorrow, forgiveness, and crucifixion; but it is formidably difficult for an innocent human being to be able to conquer the hatred of others with love, and to accept and endure an unjustified bodily crucifixion at their hands.
– The Second Coming of Christ, pg. 1484

Then, as reported in Luke 23:49, *"Jesus cried out in a loud voice, 'Father into Thy hands I commend My spirit'."* Or, as in John 19:30, with the final comment, *"It is finished,"* Jesus bowed his head and "gave up the ghost." At that moment the veil of the temple was rent in two, from top to bottom. Yogananda notes that symbolically this represented the tearing away of the veil of mystery that hides the ultimate truth of life beyond death.

What Jesus did with Lazarus was one form of resurrection, but what he demonstrated after his own death was a far greater achievement. Here, he showed the lifting of consciousness beyond all the levels of vibratory creation and then merged his Self with the Absolute Spirit.

Yogananda, with his Hindu perspective, saw deep significance in Jesus' comment that he would rise again after three days. This did not refer to physical time, but rather to his ability to initiate three consecutive phases of vibratory shift—from the physical to astral, astral to causal, and then causal into Cosmic Consciousness.

The capacity for ascension, with intention, has frequently been referred to in the ancient Vedic texts and is an ability the great rishis have achieved as well. It is considered part of their spiritual science and there are many well-documented examples of it. Those realized yogis and ascended Masters, such as Jesus, who have freed the soul from astral and causal realms and aligned with the Spirit are then able to take up the body or cast it aside at will.

On Easter Morning, the first disciple to see Jesus was Mary Magdalene. To her, he says, *"Touch me not; for I am not yet ascended...."* (John 2:19) Yogananda notes that here was work that needed to be done: *"to unloose, with the supreme soul-science of liberation, the knots of life and consciousness that both enabled and resulted from his earthly incarnation.* (The Second Coming of Christ, pg. 1501)

Again from the Hindu perspective, this would mean that when meeting Mary, Jesus had not yet worked out all the entangling interactions of the three *gunas* imprinted in his astral and causal bodies. Jesus had yet to burn these away together with all the karmic seeds, which had arisen from his "cause and effect action" while in human form. Initially, he would be occupied with removing them from the astral body, and then the causal body.

Jesus appeared later that day to two disciples who did not recognize him until he broke bread with them that evening. That same evening, he *materialized* amongst them in a room in Jerusalem. Eight days later he spontaneously appeared, again. And it was there that Thomas touched him *physically* and recognized the injuries of the crucifixion. Forty days later, Jesus appeared to his disciples and ate with them, a physical act.

The ascension is seen as the final transformation witnessed by the disciples. *"So then after the Lord had spoken unto them, he was received up into heaven and sat on the right hand of God."* (Mark 16:20) Yogananda writes that while Jesus was born in a human body, crucified and resurrected, he did not re-create a body to remain confined in it. His ascension demonstrated the omnipresence of the light of Christ Consciousness—a reflection of Cosmic Consciousness that is throughout all Creation.

> *"Through the spiritual eye, the worshiper can behold not only the Christ with form, but the formless Christ felt in the vastness of inner perception, because Christ is already present at the divine center of consciousness in all human beings.*
> – The Second Coming of Christ, pg. 1523-1524

* * * * *

Yogananda's advice for the dying

- Direct eyes upward, follow the breath.
- Appreciate all things as moving energies.
- Keep a sense of even-mindedness: Equanimity.

- Know you are not your body, but a spark of the Divine.
- Have faith in the principle of your inner continuity.

In life, Yogananda's face and bearing carried his message of love, light and power. In particular, he provided us with a deeper understanding of death as a passage and broadened our traditional Western perspective.

Yogananda himself, died quietly in California in 1953, just after concluding a speech to the Indian Ambassador at a banquet. Three weeks later, when his casket was finally closed, there was no sign of physical deterioration.

The Government of India published the following:

The ideal of love for God and service to humanity found full expression in the life of Paramahansa Yogananda...Though the major part of his life was spent outside of India, still he takes his place among our great saints. His work continues to grow and shine even more brightly, drawing people everywhere on the path of pilgrimage of the Spirit.

I was deeply moved by the Hindu perspective. It leads beyond the symbolic views of Jung and describes dying more in terms of varying qualities of energy and vibration. It also helps one gradually come to terms with all one has to leave behind. Most importantly, the Hindu perspective reinforces the notion of an archetypal process underlying death and speaks of it as a loving, learning process of spiritual growth.

* * * * *

NOTES

1. In his beautiful book, *"Life after Death,"* Deepak Chopra explores the Vedanta descriptions of the multiple sheaths (vibrations) of consciousness that exist throughout the Universe. Within humans, these sheaths are the (1) Physical body (2) Prana or life force (which joins us to nature) (3) Mind (feelings, sensations, memories, social conditioning) (4) Ego and intellect (identity, attachments) (5) 'Body of bliss' (the basic vibration, the lighted Presence behind all things). These sheaths (called Koshas) are wrapped around our central Self, like the layers of an onion with the central element being pure consciousness (Body of bliss). In death, we are shifting our attention from one level to another. Most

stay blocked in the Ego vibration with its fixed grooves of thought and behavior. It may take many lifetimes to resolve those issues.

2. Definition of Terms

Astral: Man's subtle body of light and prana. There are several astral planes from higher to lower frequencies. Even the lowest astral plane vibrates at a higher frequency than those of the material world.

Chakras: In Yoga, the seven occult centers of life and consciousness in the spine and in the brain that enliven the physical and astral bodies.

Causal: The idea-essence that underlies the physical and astral form. When one evolves sufficiently, one sheds the physical, astral and causal body to unite with the omnipresent Spirit beyond all vibratory realms.

Karma: A Sanskrit word from Hindu scriptures, which means, "to do." The law of karma says that whatever energies we have set in motion, whether wisely or unwisely, will return to us either in this life or the next.

Karmic impulse: The force that incarnates at birth and contains all the important factors for an individual's life's purpose.

Samadhi: Occurs in meditation when the mind has withdrawn from the body senses and achieves higher, blissful states.

Samskara: Imprints left in the mind after experience.

Prana: The cosmic vibratory energy, omnipresent in the universe; pervades and sustains human life; sparks of intelligent (finer than atomic) energy.

Reincarnation: Hindu belief that human beings are compelled by the law of evolution to incarnate repeatedly; retarded by wrong actions and desires, and advanced by spiritual endeavor.

Chapter 4

TIBETAN BUDDHIST PERSPECTIVE

 I watched the sun play across the beautiful beams of the Shamballa Hall. The teacher, Andrew Holcheck, was giving his second talk of a seven-week course on Death and Dying. Andrew, a long time Buddhist practitioner, had just returned from India where he had spent time meditating in the burning ghats (cremation grounds) along the sacred Ganges. The experience had given him great clarity. He told the following story, which particularly caught my attention.

In America one evening, a woman was delayed in a long line of traffic on her return home from work. She could see by the flashing lights that there was a very serious accident up ahead. While she waited, she thought she would meditate and pray for whoever might have been hurt. An ambulance went screaming by. Eventually, the traffic cleared and she went home.

A month later a knock came at her front door. When she opened it there stood a modestly dressed, older woman.

"Several weeks ago," the woman said, "I was in a bad car accident. I felt myself lift out of my body and drift back over the line of waiting cars. I was drawn by the light I could see coming from your car. I could see that you were praying for me. I could also see your license plate. I have come to thank you."

Andrew was sharing this story to illustrate a bigger picture; one where the power of subtle energy, which underlies all life, was evident. His teaching on death was exceptional, in that he carefully interwove deep esoteric understanding with practical knowledge and he confronted us with a spectrum of experience.

As I listened to Andrew, my Western mind was first fascinated by the description of the actual physical process of dying. The key issue appeared to be our breathing. Oxygen is required for life, particularly by the brain, which uses a tremendous amount of the body's oxygen intake.

As we are dying, all the body systems begin to slow down, especially the heart and brain. The person sleeps more to conserve energy; there is little desire to eat and eventually to drink. Swallowing becomes difficult and the mouth is very dry. Increasingly, the person has trouble getting comfortable and there may be pain.

As we draw close to death, there can also be muscle spasms and convulsions. Our breathing becomes labored with long pauses. Fluid gathers in the lungs and leads to the rasping of the "death rattle." There is loss of bowel and bladder control.

"Clinical" death occurs when the breathing and heart stop. At this point, CPR and other interventions may revive us; however, "biological" death occurs 4 to 6 minutes later when the brain cells begin to die.

Andrew reviewed, during his seminars, the Tibetan Buddhist ideas about death and the afterlife. He shared the prescribed postures and breathing practices a person would use while dying. He discussed the inner processes; how the mental body goes through all manner of experiences and is visited by joyful and wrathful deities, which can arise symbolically.

He sent us on two field trips. The first was to the local funeral home. I remember looking at the stainless steel tables used in the embalming process and being told about the chemicals employed. Then, we were shown the large, cremation furnace with its potential for incredible temperatures. I wondered whether my artificial knee would be left in the dust after all that heat.

The second field trip was to a medical lab where we spent several hours with ten or twelve bodies. These had been given to medical science and we were impressed by how they were treated, with great respect, by the professionals present. The overall sense, however, was that the lifeless bodies were just intricate clay replicas of humans, like husks shed from an earlier season.

If Andrew had wanted to gradually awaken us to the contrast between matter and spirit which death ultimately means, he had provided powerful experiences.

* * * * *

I gathered further materials on the Tibetan Buddhist perspective on death (see Bibliography). I have summarized its approach through this mighty doorway, under the following headings:

(1) The Great Challenge
(2) The Framework
(3) The Dissolution Process:
    (i)   Bardo of Dying
    (ii) Bardo of Death
    (iii) Bardo of Becoming
(4) The Advice

(1) The Great Challenge

The central thesis of the Tibetan Buddhist perspective is that dying is one event in the continuity of consciousness. Death, however, is of prime importance— an event horizon where all else can dissolve, but the eternal Mind can be experienced.

Sogyal Rinpoche writes that one should take death seriously, not naively or complacently. One should bring to it an acceptance, as well as a clear understanding that suffering and pain can be part of this deep, natural process of purification. However, there is purpose to this journey.

> *When we finally know we are dying, and all other sentient beings are dying with us, we start to have a burning, almost heart-breaking sense of the fragility and preciousness of each moment and each being, and from this can grow a deep, clear, limitless compassion for all beings.*
> – The Tibetan Book of Living and Dying, pg. 187

The kindness and wisdom inherent in the Buddhist writings emphasize that there is a way through this passage. It can be helped by skillful means—by understanding what's involved and addressing its reality with devoted meditative practice.

For the Buddhist, death is the great Teacher. It demonstrates the Law of Impermanence. It is the evidence!! Death is a time of Truth. Most of us don't want to think about such irrevocable change; but this confrontation *will* happen to us all; *"The Moving Finger writes and having writ moves on..."*. Buddhists have found in death a much bigger picture—one that offers great opportunities, a time of summation, purification and possibly liberation.

A basic tenet of Tibetan Buddhism is reincarnation. Another life succeeds our current life. This is not seen as one soul appearing after another like beads on a string; rather, there is a continuity of our consciousness. The early Christian church also held this belief. Origen, one of the most influential church fathers, wrote in the 3rd century, "Each soul comes to this world reinforced by the victories or enfeebled by the defeats of its previous lives." Similarly, for the Buddhist, we all have a special energy field in our innermost subtle level of consciousness, which arises, and is supported and functionally connected to the existence that preceded it.

Buddhists understand death "in the context of the structure of Mind, itself." There exists within us "the relative mind" (of the personality) and the "clear, luminous Mind" that underlies, permeates and supports all existence. To become "realized" in the eternal, luminous Mind is the goal of the spiritual life. While this is usually only attained at the time of death by the experienced practitioner, it is available to us while we live, as Buddha exemplified. Most people however, do not achieve "realization," although great strides may be made in maturity and spiritual development.

With our "relative mind," we live in the self-object world of relationships of our everyday life. We are so immersed and identified with our relative mind that, for the most part, we live unaware of the great ocean of Awareness we are surrounded by—the eternal, luminous Mind. Our "relative mind" connects to the appearances within our third dimensional world reality. It gets us across the street without being hit by the bus; it talks with our children at dinner, and registers the inputs within our body. In short, it relates to "the Other." We orient ourselves through the "relative mind" and are connected to our three-dimensional world through its feedback.

Dying brings us up against all these "Others." It confronts the "relative mind's" perceptions of its realities and attachments with the need to let go.

(2) The Framework

For the Buddhist, dying is a dance of withdrawal from the physical basis of perception. Loss of the body throws us more and more deeply into our subjective world. There is an essential optimism about our ultimate spiritual destination within the Buddhist philosophy and this informs the details of the dying process.

Another basic tenet in Buddhist thought is the notion of "bardo." A "bardo" describes a gap, an intermediate or a transition period in the journey of life and death. There are two basic types of bardos:—conceptual and— nonconceptual bardo.

The conceptual bardo is an experience of a certain duration of time—marked by a beginning, a sense of continuity and an end. The nonconceptual bardo is the *immediate* experience at the end of one moment and before the next begins. It is NOW—if we can be aware of it, we have an opportunity to recognize the *fundamental nature of our own Mind*. If we can be "Here Now," we can abide in its stillness; and sense, with great clarity, absolute Truth, the actual Reality.

There are several schools of thought in Buddhist traditions on the bardos and many variations in their maps. From the Vajrayana Buddhist, Dzogchen Ponlop describes six bardos: three sets of experiences in life and three sets in the death process. The latter are called "bardo of dying," "bardo of death" and "bardo of becoming" (being drawn into the next life). The following descriptions come from his Vajrayana perspective.

(3) The Dissolution Process:

(i) Bardo of Dying

The complex, ordered process of death occurs through the coarse body, the subtle energy body and the nature of mind. These systems are all interdependent and so each is gradually affected in the dying process.

As a particular system dissolves, we first experience an increase and then a decrease in the function and qualities of that part. For example, the person might "brighten" consciously or suddenly speak more clearly, just before dying. Interestingly, as the mind becomes less connected to the physical body there are flashes of inner light that foretell the approach of luminosity (the ultimate nature of the Mind).

a. Coarse Body Dissolution

From the Vajrayana Buddhist point of view, there are certain fundamental energies found in the central core along the spine, which nourish the body functions. Energy flows from this central core through branches into the chakra systems, filling them with life's vital energy or prana. As the dying process begins all the body systems supported by this energy start to decline. Energy is released from the chakras and flows back into the central channel. Dissolution occurs gradually and sequentially. Body and mind disintegrate from the grossest to the subtlest in this order:

Stage One: We feel heavy, with a crushing weight on the chest; there is a great loss of physical strength and our balance is compromised; even our mind begins to feel heavy. Our sight is dimming as if there is not enough light in the room. Dream sequences may pass through our minds. The chakra at the navel center, which binds the energy flowing through that area, begins to dissolve.

Stage Two: Our mind can become restless; emotions are easily provoked. Our consciousness becomes vague and "foggy." Our field of awareness may register clouds, like smoke or steam, and there is a sense of emptiness. Now the heart chakra begins to dissolve.

Stage Three: While the extremities are cooling there is an increase, and then a decrease in body heat. Our limbs stiffen. Our sense of smell is gone. We do not recognize people. Here is where, for some, there may appear sparks of light as the luminous aspects of Mind increase.

Stage Four: As our breathing becomes more difficult, with long inhalations and some rattling in the throat, the eyes may roll upward and remain there longer. Taste and touch senses have dissolved. After three long, final exhalations both heart and breathing cease.

These first four stages are grouped together as they are considered direct shifts in the physical basis of the life. The map of consciousness held by the Vajrayana school is very complex; there is not a single consciousness but a collection of consciousnesses, all affected at different stages in the dying process.

b. Stage Five: Dissolution of the Subtle Body

Dzogchen Ponlop pursues one of the finer types of consciousness that the Vajrayan school of Tibetan Buddhism is interested in. He describes in detail, how, in normal life, the relative or conceptual mind (one type of consciousness) arises from the more fundamental nature of our Mind—its pure awareness or luminosity. The relative or conceptual mind sees and considers an object (perhaps a cup). It apprehends the cup; engages in thoughts and feelings about the cup and then allows the perception of the cup to dissolve naturally back into the original ground luminosity. This is like a wave that emerges from the surface of the ocean only to sink back again. The conceptual mind is in perpetual motion, back and forth, arising, abiding and ceasing.

Dzogchen Ponlop uses very specific words to describe this process. From non-conceptuality (pure awareness), the relative world arises as "appearance," moves though "increase"(comprehension) and then to "attainment" (absorption back into the original ground of mind.) This is an interesting choice of words and again reinforces the Buddhist focus on the eternal, luminous Mind from which all arises.

When we are dying, the process of "appearance," "increase" and "attainment" is reversed. Gradually, during the stages that were noted above, there is a diminished ability to apprehend and engage with external objects. For example, we no longer identify or connect with a cup held before us. It is no longer my yellow cup, then no longer a yellow cup, or then not even a cup.

After the loss of gross physical functions, what is termed "subtle inner breathing" continues for about twenty minutes. Now, there are the other dissolutions on the level of the subtle body, particularly those of emotions.

At this time, the mind is very confused and unstable; the whole life can be reflected and magnified.

Hallucinations may arise from "karmic seeds" i.e. those habituated tendencies with negative or positive themes we developed during our life. With less and less connection with the body, these visions are intense and appear real. Their dramas powerfully impact us. Yet this is a key moment; if we are trained we can appreciate that here is the mirror nature of mind, itself.

Then comes the final dissolution of this dualistic mind. Now the five senses that directly perceive objects and visions and the discursive mind (that thinks) all dissolve into formless awareness—into "space."

During the bardo of dying there is, actually, a second process of subtle energies moving through the stages of "appearance," " increase" and "attainment." The life force energies we receive from both parents at conception live in our body as two luminous bright lights, called "bindus." The masculine energy inherited from the father dwells at the crown chakra at the top the central energy (spinal) channel, and is called the white bindu. The feminine or mother energy resides at the base of the central channel and is called the red bindu.

As we die, these energies begin to more towards each other and eventually unite in the heart. Initially, as consciousness begins its descent, it is experienced at the crown chakra, as luminous and white, "like moonlight shining in a cloudless sky." Our awareness becomes very clear and all thoughts of aggression cease. This phase is known as "appearance."

Then the red bindu from the lower level begins to move upward and is experienced as luminous and red, "like sunlight shining in a cloudless sky." There is an experience here of bliss and all thoughts of desire are now released. This phase is known as "increase."

When these energies reach the heart, one enters a darkness said to be "like a cloudless sky without sunlight, moonlight or starlight." The mind is free of thoughts and ignorance. This state is known as "full attainment."

Now the inner subtle respiration stops and consciousness dissolves into space. If the mind has not been trained through practice, one loses all awareness at this point. The screen becomes dark. The bardo of dying is complete and this particular life has ended.

Dzogchen Ponlop describes this juncture as follows:

"Subsequently, space itself dissolves into the ground luminosity. At that time we arrive at the stage of full attainment. All notions of self and other, existence or non-existence, good and bad are completely dissolved — and nonconceptual awareness wisdom manifests fully."

– Mind Beyond Death, pg. 137

Sogyal Rinpoche summarizes it as follows:

"I have found that the easiest way to understand what is happening during the process of dying, with its outer and inner dissolution, is as a gradual development and dawning of ever more subtle levels of consciousness. Each one emerges upon the successive dissolution of the constituents of body and mind, as the process moves gradually toward the revelation of the very subtlest consciousness of all: the Ground Luminosity or Clear Light."
– The Tibetan Book of Living and Dying, pg. 25

(ii) Bardo of Death

The bardo of death is considered to occur with the final dissolution of dualistic consciousness. As noted, at this point there is an experience of a vast openness of clear sky, with no object, just a great radiant clarity of awareness (described above as the Ground Luminosity or Clear Light). If, during one's lifetime, one has stabilized the mind through meditation, one is able to register the great emptiness of the moment. There is recognition that this is the ultimate state—the rising radiant Luminosity of the Buddha nature.

The Tibetan Buddhists believe that even if we have failed to recognize the underlying reality of Mind during our lifetime, it is possible to do so at this moment; however such recognition is a very challenging task. Sogyal Rinpoche writes, *"most are totally unprepared for its sheer immensity, the vast and subtle depth of It's naked simplicity."* Without preparation, we tend to react instinctively with all our old reflexes and shrink away.

Now, however, we will be confronted by archetypal and primal energies arising from the fundamental Mind. These energies, referred to as "the peaceful and wrathful deities," represent qualities inherent in the primordial wisdom of Mind. We experience a mirroring of their natural activity. If we can consider those images, not as real external phenomena, but coming from emotions and thoughts of basic mind, we can retain our steadiness.

The ability to do this requires deep practice. Even those who have meditated extensively during their lifetime often do not have the ability to break through the barriers that keep us from realizing the real nature of the Ground Luminosity. Wise guidance from an experienced teacher is necessary.

(iii) Bardo of Becoming

Gradually a perception of dawn arises again out of the great ocean of light and energy. There are several subtle levels to this process only detectable with specific Buddhist practices. The mind and its fundamental nature now re-emerge with an ability to assess the possibilities for another life; one, which offers further opportunities for spiritual growth.

(4) The Advice

> *"We need to allow the person to die in silence and serenity. Peaceful death is really an essential human right, more essential, perhaps, even than the right to vote or the right to justice. It is a right on which all religious traditions tell us a great deal depends, for the well-being and spiritual future of the dying person."*
> The Tibetan Book of Living and Dying, pg. 186

If one has been wise enough to become a disciplined Buddhist practitioner during one's lifetime, one has prepared well for the three bardos of death. Sogyal Rinpoche says that when we have come to understand the difference between our relative or conceptual mind and the pure, pristine Awareness that underlies it, which is intelligent, cognizant, radiant and always awake, we come to see death very differently.

The Tibetan Buddhist perspective would say about the dying process that when the time comes:

- Meditate.
- Work with one's mind to remain calm and clear even though that may be interrupted at times.
- Maintain a positive state of mind with kindness to self and other.
- Transform the fear; "letting go" eases all transitions.
- Be aware that one's last thought at the moment of death exerts a powerful influence on the process.
- Focus on the crown chakra. In the midst of all the changes that come, simply rest in a relaxed and spacious mind.
- Set one's intention to open to one's fundamental Buddha nature. Obscured as it is by "the storage faculty" of mind and all past karmic seeds, there lies the Light-Illumination of our fundamental nature.

We in the West have received great gifts from the East and only recently have begun to appreciate them.

As I explored Tibetan Buddhism, I kept seeing in my mind long lines of wise practitioners, stretching back hundreds of years, sitting in meditation and allowing layer upon layer of profound understanding to arise.

The wise ones, who wrote the books I have cited, spoke of the difficulty in conveying the reality of these states of mind through writing. The words would seem so remote and conceptual. Then I read an anecdote from the Dalai Lama that brought the "feeling" of the Buddhist perspective a little closer.

He had been taken very ill and was being rushed, in great pain, to an Indian hospital. On the way, they saw a crippled child with a rusty crutch and a very old man dying alone at the side of the road. The Dalai Lama spoke of the flood of compassion he felt at that moment for all the suffering in this world; how that compassion diminishes the fright about one's own pain; how it brings courage and humanity to one's heart, and how, in a paradoxical way, it lends encouragement even in the face of death.

Chapter 5

REFLECTIONS ON REINCARNATION

Many years ago I found myself in the New Mexico desert. Abrupt changes in my personal life led me to deeply question my relationships. At the suggestion of a friend, I signed up for 5 days of individual sessions at the Light Institute in Galesteo. This center is well known for its facilitators, skilled in past life regressions. The sessions ran for 3-4 hours each day and were followed by cranial sacral work. This type of massage of the head helps the flow of energy up and down the spine, which assists in integrating the emotional material that arises in the sessions.

It was a profound experience for me. Every day, prompted by the gentle encouragement of the facilitator to relax more deeply into my inner images, I found story after story emerging. The facilitator's question "and then what happened?" would lead to more images. Dramas of love, loss, betrayal, idealism, shame, degradation, idealistic missions and low life tumbled out, hour after hour. They ranged from a primitive life fighting for survival on a South American savanna to a European Crusader to a dispirited Arapahoe watching the relentless push of the white man.

Especially surprising was what would surface with the question, "Who, in your present life might that other person be?" Each story drew to a close with the questions: "How did you die in that life?" and then "What did the Soul learn?"

Every evening, I would return to my room and fall into bed, exhausted. The sense of inter-weaving dramas, one joined with the next like a sine wave, was strong. I was shocked and humbled to experience the "shadow" lives I had lived. I saw the processes of my own dying over and over again, some easy, some hard, some lingering, some abruptly cut off.

I emerged from that week with these conclusions: I could be *anybody* and had been. I felt loosened from my identity and my context. It was not random, however; there was a thread of continuity. Some underlying "conscience" in my life pulled for justice and balance. I was and am responsible for my choices. The Soul within is the Teacher.

Because of that intense week, the following ideas made a lot of sense to me.

In the book, *Zen: Merging of East and West,* Roshi Philllip Kapleau converses with a number of workshop participants. In response to a question raised about death, the Roshi explained that it is far more important to find out who we are now, when we are alive, than what happens after death. However, he noted, that in a culture such as ours, which has so much denial about death, exploration of the question could lead to a renewed interest in the quality of our present life.

So Roshi Kapleau gave the following explanation. First, he said, we have to consider that in the Zen Buddhist perspective there are, within us, *nine* levels of consciousness. The first six levels are the five senses and the thought processes of our mind. These arrive with our birth and vanish with our death.

Levels *seven, eight* and *nine* of consciousness do not perish. Each has a different function in the continuity of our deeper knowing.

Level seven: called "manas" consciousness, is self-aware; it is the seat of discrimination (rooted in desire and craving). It acts like conveyer agent of accumulated experience (from levels 1-6) to level eight.

Level eight: called *relative* "alaya" consciousness, records and retains all our actions and thoughts. These, each in turn, change the quality of our repository consciousness. This leads to new seeds, which become the basis of the actions and behaviors of the next life. Karma comes from these ever accumulating seeds in an on-going process.

Level nine: called *absolute* "alaya" consciousness, is the pure, formless Self-consciousness and our True Nature. It is the limitless ocean in which each individual life is a wave on the surface.

In the chart provided, the levels are arranged as a progression. Life 1 is followed by Life 2, which carries "the seeds" from the stored experiences of Life 1 (found in level 8a). These seeds will influence Life 2. Then the accumulated responses of Life 2 (found in level 8b) will influence the next incarnation (Life 3). The quality of Level 9 of our true formless Nature will gradually be revealed over these progressions.

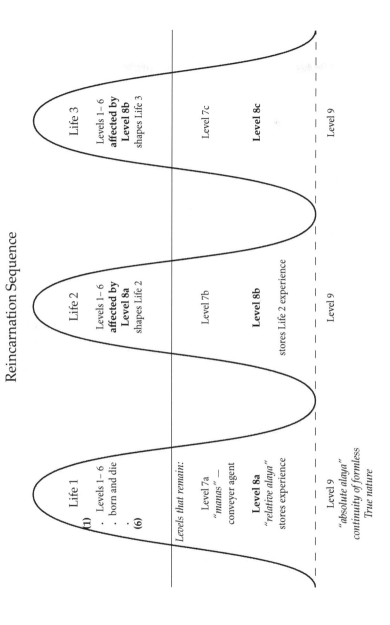

Reincarnation Sequence

Life 1

(1)
· Levels 1–6
· born and die
·
(6)

Levels that remain:

Level 7a
"manas" —
conveyer agent

Level 8a
"relative alaya"
stores experience

Level 9
"absolute alaya"
continuity of formless
True nature

Life 2

Levels 1–6
**affected by
Level 8a**
shapes Life 2

Level 7b

Level 8b

stores Life 2 experience

Level 9

Life 3

Levels 1–6
**affected by
Level 8b**
shapes Life 3

Level 7c

Level 8c

Level 9

Until I sat down to write this book, I had forgotten about the experiences I had had in the desert so many years ago. At the time, they had drawn me to study the work of Alice Bailey.

I was very fortunate to meet Donna Mitchell-Moniak of the Spirit Fire Institute. Donna was a life-long student of Alice Bailey and the insights of The Tibetan. Her workshops confronted us with the habitual patterns of our mind and the behaviors that result from them. The teachings also confirmed that after we die, we will find ourselves in the same mind-stream in which we habitually lived: so there was an incentive to grow in awareness. Donna's meditations, in particular, encouraged us to hold all things in the spaciousness of the mind's Stillness.

Chapter 6

AGELESS WISDOM PERSPECTIVE

 Another extensive description of the timing and process of death is provided by the esoteric teachings of Djwal Khul, also called Master D.K., or The Tibetan. These teachings, referred to as The Ageless Wisdom Tradition, are found in the twenty-four volumes of the Blue Books of Alice Bailey, published by the Lucis Trust from 1919 to 1949.

Here are a few phrases from this wise perspective which describe the dying process:

When one has obtained the objective there is no more aspiration. An adequate vibration and point of balance has been achieved.
   – Cosmic Fire, pg. 428

The Thinker on his own plane withdraws his attention from his little system within the three worlds and gathers to himself all his forces, and then physical plane existence comes to an end.
   – Cosmic Fire, pg. 85

The soul is persistent and deathless, the form is
changing and doomed to die. For the progress of
the soul of the individual and the soul of humanity,
death is inevitable, good and necessary.
 – Externalization of the Hierarchy, pg. 115

Here is a most comforting thought from this ancient philosophy. When the deep Spirit within us knows that *our life project* is completed, the dying process begins.

All quoted phrases suggest that life is meaningful, purposeful and carries a design that was implicit from the beginning. The phrases also reveal a sense of rhythm about life, as a continuous unfolding process. The view of the human psyche is that it is multidimensional and composed of different qualities of energy or vibration.

The Western world is only beginning to open to these ideas. Again, as Carl Jung has written, *"modern man has no idea how complex we are, having lost the basic understanding of our deeper nature."*

What would accepting our own deeper nature mean? Consider these additional words from The Tibetan:

Can you picture the time when the process of death,
clearly recognized and welcomed by man, could
be described in the simple phrase, "The time has
come when my soul's attractive force requires that

I relinquish and restore my body to the place from whence it came"?
– Esoteric Healing, pg. 427

It is time to develop a more adequate form for the use of Spirit."
–Esoteric Healing, pg. 131

As in the other traditions, the Ancient Wisdom Perspective also elaborates the inner dimensions of the human psyche. It notes that these dimensions nest together, are energetic, and each carry unique qualities and capacities. The higher frequencies of our being are increasingly less materialized.[1]

The Tibetan considers death in the context of two great planetary processes: *involution* and *evolution*. With involution, light and life are poured into a vessel (the body form) on the physical plane. In evolution, light and life are withdrawn from the physical plane and returned to the Center from whence they came. This process affects all forms: ants, man and planets.

Life is inherently dualistic. Two major streams of energy enter the body to produce its activity, quality and type of expression. On one level, the soul acquires a physical body adequate to its requirements. It energizes it with *etheric* energy for the duration of its needs.

On another level, the soul puts forth the stream of individual consciousness, the "desire" mind of the personality.

Dying, notes The Tibetan, is one of our most practiced activities and begins when an impulse of Will is sent by the Monad to the soul. This "call" begins a sequence of processes called (1) Restitution (2) Elimination and (3) Integration.

Process of Restitution

"Restitution" means to restore, to put back what one has borrowed or pay back a debt. Now, in dying, one returns the material one has used to where it has come from.

Restitution moves through several general phases.

Phase 1: On the physical level, the etheric body, which has interpenetrated and supported all the cells, does two things:

a)   Restores the atoms of matter to the dense planetary life.

b)   Itself returns to the general reservoir of planetary energies.

Phase 2: Releases the desire mind of the personality; the grasping quality that reaches for the third-dimensional world (referred to in these teachings as "the world of glamor").

The process of restitution follows a well-ordered sequence of events:

(1) The soul sounds forth a word of withdrawal (as a vibration)

- This vibration affects the blood stream, the nervous system and the endocrine system.

- A vibration runs along the nadis (the etheric energies that underlie all the nervous system).

- The blood stream changes because of a secretion from the glands. This substance affects the heart.

- A psychic tremor is set up, which, starting with the eyes, loosens the nadis from the nervous system.

(2) A Pause

- There is a pause of shorter or longer duration. This allows for the gradual loosening process of the nadis to go smoothly. The dying person relaxes. There is a willingness to let go and an inability to make a mental effort.

(3) Two processes are going on (under the Law of Attraction)

- The physical body is steadily being released from the integrating potency of the vital body by the action of the nadis. It begins to feel the pull of the great reservoir of Earth matter itself.

- The vital body is preparing for its exit, which varies with the level of development of the soul. The light of the soul is being withdrawn.

(4) A Second Pause

- Of short or long duration depending on the will of the soul. Sometimes death may not be part of the immediate plan or the attachment to the physical element is so powerful the person fights the dying process. In which case, the second pause may be longer.

- Etheric body gradually disperses, leaving the body vacated and the vital body of the individual detached. As the etheric and vital energies are withdrawing from the heart, there is a brilliant flaring–up of light.

(5) Subtle body: Freed from restitution

- Now free of the physical body the person remains themself; untouched and untrammelled; but responsive to the quality of their astral and mental body and the voice (guidance) of their soul.

- The vacating of the physical body and the complete dissolution of the etheric body happen at the same time. Much of what happens next depends on the person's level of spiritual development.

The Art of Elimination

The process of elimination reflects The Tibetan's understanding that spiritual evolution eventually requires removing the controlling influence of the *"threefold lower man"* (the physical, etheric and astral energies).

The Tibetan describes people at three levels of development, each of which has a different experience immediately after death. At this point, there is no physical brain. What one can register depends on "the innate activity of the inner man and his peculiar state of apprehension and of appreciation."
– Esoteric Healing, pg. 488

The three levels of development are:

Kamic: the vast majority of people whose emotional natures are strongly reactive. As they die, their souls exit from the solar plexus.

Kama-manasic: balanced people with integrated, kind personalities given to service in the community. As they die, their souls usually leave through the heart.

Manasic: advanced people, disciples and initiates who have been mainly focused in the mental realm. As they die, their souls exit from the crown.

* * * * *

For the Kamic people, there is little for them to do immediately after death as they don't yet have the consciousness to release themselves from the other states of consciousness that still contain them. They persist in the astral realm until drawn back into the re-incarnational cycle.

The Kama-manasic people are as much aware and alert to their environment as they were to the physical plane when they were alive. ("Plane" here, again, means a state of consciousness, not a location.) Such people exist within the astral plane knowing the theme of that environment and their emotional desires. The level of the astral plane they find themselves in corresponds to the maturity they achieved in physical existence. A characteristic of their astral plane is that their thoughts quickly manifest forms.

The Manasic people, after death, carry a high level of awareness of love and aspiration. The astral quality will dissolve more readily for them and they will feel the pull toward the point of radiant light of the mental body. This is the doorway towards "the Monad."

> *However, all, immediately after death, will be in an astral body on an astral plane. At this moment, there will be direct contact with one's soul, which allows the person to see "the experience of the past incarnation spread before him like a map."*
> – Esoteric Healing, pg. 491

The clarity provided here by the soul opens a perceptual doorway: one sees all the consequences of one's past attitudes and actions. Now the person's soul isolates three major conditioning factors or "seeds" that hold the key to shape the future incarnation. They are:

Seed One: the nature of the physical environment, which will influence the needed field of experience for the next life.

Seed Two: the quality of the etheric body and the chakras; emphasizing those, which will be most active (Ray structure).

Seed Three: the astral or emotional keynote, which will bring the person into relation with those he previously loved or with whom he had close contact.

> *"The familiar and the loved will still remain the familiar and the loved, because the relation has been closely established over many incarnations."*
> – Esoteric Healing, pg. 493

The Process of Integration

The Tibetan says that after many lifetimes of death and rebirth and practicing the art of elimination, the mind becomes more potent and incisive. There is an evolutionary timetable, which evokes a greater ability to discriminate.

While in transition on "the inner side," one begins to realize that continuity of consciousness is a fact and reincarnation is inevitable. It is now understood that incarnation in the physical world provides opportunities for emotional maturation. Aware of the qualities one has already achieved, there is more deliberate choice of the substances needed for rebirth, i.e. parents and life circumstances.

The emotional maturation deepens because of the ongoing integration of the personality with the soul. The Tibetan writes that the soul exists "on its own higher plane" where it carries great light, love and wisdom. The soul "puts down" a fragment of itself into the personality and as the personality opens to it over many lifetimes, the soul has more influence. Now consciousness and conscience "awaken" and there is greater sense of responsibility. The person is considered to be on "the Path of the Initiate," that of the "Lighted Way."

The advanced person now identifies more with their soul, which becomes evident in their life. In the after-death realm, there is a growing awareness of the Eternal Now and that there are richer and fuller experiences available in the esoteric realms than when incarnated in physical life. A student of the Ageless Wisdom tradition learns of the various higher Initiations that lie on that path of evolution. They, as disciples, recognize it as an ordered process of continual surrender and higher integration. They willingly and more quickly relinquish the lesser and more constraining sheaths of consciousness after death.

> *It is because we in the Western cultures don't think*
> *that the soul has a purpose that reincarnation (with*
> *its understanding of our ancient heredities and*
> *environments) is ignored and death appears*
> *so meaningless.*
> – Esoteric Healing, pg. 436

I was deeply moved by the amazing vista of higher awareness and purpose that unfolds in the Ancient Wisdom tradition. Just as the soul gradually takes over the integrated personality, the soul itself is eventually absorbed into the higher illumined Monadic vehicle. Such is the accomplishment of the great spiritual masters who continue to be of service to mankind in and beyond incarnation.

Reflecting on this material I thought about Jung's most basic notion—our life unfolds under the direction of the Self (Jung's term for the soul and Spirit).

Here, again, it is affirmed that within us, there is a dynamic, which is quietly at work throughout our lives.

In his teachings, The Tibetan has laid out a map, not only how our Being matures, but also how it passes through phases of dying and continues to moves on. While the map is conceptual, it encourages the reader to explore the experiences of the afterlife with courage and equanimity.

Advice when dying:
- Know thyself to be the undying One.

- Control thy mind (for through that mind the undying One can be known).

- Learn that the form is but the veil, which hides the lighted splendor of Divinity.

- Realize that the One Life pervades all forms, so that there is no death, no distress, and no separation.

- Detach thyself therefore, from the form side and come to Me, so dwelling in the place where Light and Life are found. Thus illusion ends.

- Use a mantra such as "Father, into Thy hands I commend my Spirit" or "Lord, now let Thy servant depart in peace."

  – A Treatise on White Magic, pg.458-459

NOTES

1. Our Multidimensional Bodies (typically, each plane has seven further sub-layers):

Physical: The most basic is our physical body with its biological structures and processes.

Etheric: The energetic layer that supports all the physical cells and systems is called "the etheric layer." This living, flowing river of "prana" or life force energy has been described as a fine network of fiery threads which also sustain our emotional, lower and higher mental bodies. We, in the West, are just now appreciating its presence in acupuncture, homeopathy, cranial sacral work and other New Age healing modalities.

Astral: Sometimes referred to as the emotional body or "desire mind," this layer carries strong elements of our identity and attachments. As one aspect of our personality, it anchors the preferences, likes and dislikes that make up our motivations.

Mental: The lower levels of the mental body are connected to the five senses and are concerned with objective thinking, concept formation and conclusions. The higher levels of the mental body are intuitional and bring in those insights and understandings of spiritual principles from our soul. Gradual maturation develops the Spiritual Triad (see below) and its potential for further Light.

Intuitional or Buddhic: From this high level, comes the source of divine knowledge, and psychic ability. These energies can be seen within the human aura. The Tibetan pictures two locations of the soul. One (sometimes called "the jiva") is incarnated into our body in the three-dimensional world; the other is not incarnated, but is transcendent. This idea is key! We are continually challenged with opportunities for the unfolding of greater awareness of the transcendent soul.

Atma: The pure soul, which carries the intention of our Monad.

Monad: The individualized spark of the Divine Spirit. While it is distinct from The Source, it generates our soul and more materialized energies.

The Spiritual Triad: Lies within the overall field of awareness of the human soul. It comes into existence when aspects of the Mental, Intuitional and Atma energies have matured enough to combine their forces.

Ray Structures: Overarching and supporting our fundamental human consciousness are seven primary Rays
of pure energy, which arise from pure Light. They each
have a specific frequency and quality.

Ray 1 (Power, Will, Purpose)
Ray 2 (Love-Wisdom)
Ray 3 (Creative Intelligence)
Ray 4 (Harmony through Conflict)
Ray 5 (Science and Knowledge)
Ray 6 (Devotion)
Ray 7 (Synthesis)

Ray qualities are expressed through us over our
lifetime. The various aspects of our psyche can carry
different Ray structures. For example, our soul may be
informed by the characteristics of Ray 2, while Ray 5
influences our personality.

Chapter 7

CULTURAL QUESTIONS

Some moments are printed indelibly. I remember sitting with my partner, Ed, in the park looking across the Denver City Lake at the shining mountains to the west. We were both silent. What lay ahead?

We were several blocks away from the University of Colorado Medical Center. Ed was due, within the hour, to begin chemotherapy for his leukemia. "It's a rare and deadly variety," the doctor had said. "The survival rate is about 15%."

"However, we want to try an experimental protocol, if you agree. It is a specially potent cocktail of chemicals."

Ed, who was a doctor himself, agreed to the trial. He was 60 years-old and still actively practicing. It seemed like the right decision at the time.

Who else, every day, opens the door to that great Unknown? Ed became so very sick. He was in the hospital for twelve weeks, five of which were in intensive care. In the course of that time, he lost 65 pounds, had a bowel blockage, a bleeding ulcer, a mild stroke and heart failure. At one time, the intensive care doctor said to me, "We do not know what more to do." I brought in several non-traditional energy healers to help.

During this long process, there were two otherworldly events. One night, having returned to our mountain home, I fell into an exhausted sleep. Suddenly there was a tremendous crash. I sat up with a start. It was exactly midnight. There, scattered across my bed covers, were thousands of tiny crystals of glass. The large tumbler by my bed had shattered. A voice had said, "You must let Ed go on his own soul's journey!" I quickly called the hospital, thinking he had died. There was no change in his condition.

What was the force that broke the drinking glass? Where did that Voice come from and why was the message delivered so forcefully? It felt like a lesson I had to learn, but one I was totally unwilling to accept.

I was with Ed when he had one of his major crises. They were transferring him from a gurney to the hospital bed when his heart stopped. "Code Blue" instantly summoned the staff. They managed to get his heart beating again. They allowed me to spend the night with him.

Early the next morning, Ed called to me, "Did you see that?" He was wreathed in smiles. He went on "I got up out of my body and went to the door. There were three tall, glowing figures there. They asked me if I wanted to go with them. I looked back at my poor, tired body still in the bed and I saw you dozing there. I said 'no, not yet'—then 'zoom', I was back in my body."

Ed was elated by the experience and for several days recounted it to every medical person who came into his room. It changed his perspective. Always a kindly man, he became totally openhearted.

After the twelve weeks of treatment and recovery, Ed's doctor said to me "He's very weak, but you need to get him out of here before the hospital kills him." Collecting Ed's few belongings, I bundled him up and we left. As we drove out of town, Ed asked if we could stop at the first park we could find. He fell softly out of the van and lay gratefully on the grass.

Ed was very exhausted for several months, but he did gradually recover enough for us to travel to places he yet wanted to see. He was in remission for eighteen months. When the leukemia came back, he declined further treatment and died quietly one winter's night in our mountain home.

There are so many questions that arise, in this all too common tale of illness and decline. What were the costs of Ed's choice? What were the trade-offs?

Jung would say that our Western world has not realized that death is the most fundamental part of human existence. Here, because it is a subject to be avoided, we have sanitized it. Our advancing technology is marvelous and every day some one rejoices at its capability. However, as noted before, when it comes to the natural cycles of life, technology has a shadow side.

In his remarkable book, *Being Mortal,* Atul Gawande asks—when will we recognize that after a certain point, life is fragile? He writes, "Our reluctance to honestly examine the experience of aging and dying has increased the harm we inflict on people and denied them the basic comforts they most need. Lacking a coherent view of how people might live successfully all the way to their very end, we have allowed our fates to be controlled by the imperatives of medicine, technology and strangers."

Gawande writes that part of the difficulty is that it is hard to determine who is actually dying. Most people today, die after a long struggle with a debilitating condition. Death is certain, but the timing is not. Many opt for the most aggressive medical interventions possible, thinking it will give them years, although frequently, it only gives them months.

It is the overwhelming anxiety we feel in the face of death that creates such pressure. Gawande goes on to note that in cultures and times where the art of dying has been cultivated, there are customs, texts and prayers. There are prescribed behaviors, such as reaffirming one's faith and reconciling troubled relationships. There are questions posed to the dying to help them find the right frame of mind.

Mostly, Gawande says, in our modern Western culture, the more we can accept death as a natural part of our life's cycle the more we will focus on ways we want to shape the end of our story. Then our priorities become clearer to ourselves.

Three months after the problematic mammogram indicating that I had invasive cancer, I had surgery, a double lumpectomy on one side and a single lumpectomy on the other. The oncologist said I was too old for chemotherapy but he was sending me for five weeks of radiation. "Wait!" I said. I showed him research that reported the statistical results of radiation for women over the age of 70, with my level of breast cancer, were not much different than those who had no radiation at all. So I declined. I am now in my eighty-second year. Time to summarize, so many things.

Chapter 8

SUMMARY

 All five perspectives that I explored: Jung, Grof, the Hindu, the Vajrayana Buddhist, and the Ageless Wisdom of The Tibetan, offer good advice on how to approach death, and what one might expect on the other side. After emerging from the readings, I felt "heartened." Yes, there are realistic fears! Dying is *such a change*—literally like falling off a cliff. There are so many good-byes! And sadness! And I know I still fear the possible physical discomfort and pain of the process.

On the other hand, I hear the advice that calls for patience with the dissolution inherent in the journey. The dissolution does end. And as The Tibetan noted there is the sense of expansion and liberation that occurs after death. Even the intuitive Emmanuel echoed: *"Death is like taking off a tight shoe."* Rainer Maria Rilke's poetic words were:

"So fetch me from this place that has cramped me many a day;
So that at last I can stretch myself and sing and play."

(Such a paradox, since it could just as well be the prayer of the babe, nine months in-utero.)

The three Oriental perspectives I looked into— Hindu, Tibetan Buddhist and the Ancient Wisdom Tradition have these beliefs in common:

- We have an eternal essence
- There is continuity of consciousness after death
- There is within us, a series of subtle bodies existing like sheaths of increasing refinement
- There are intrinsic maturational processes
- Ultimately, we return to the Source

I felt reassured that these conclusions were reached by deep meditation and reflection of generations of Hindu rishis and Tibetan Buddhists. The basic ideas also align with the mystics of old, as well as our present day consciousness researchers. They are, with the exception of reincarnation, the bedrock of the Christian thought.

What heartens me most is the deepened sense of the soul's journey. Whether it is Jung, Grof, Yogananda,

Dzogchen Ponlop, Sogyal Rinpoche or The Tibetan, the message is the same. The soul's journey is archetypal, set out in the stars with organization and meaning. It has always been there and will always be there: progressive, beckoning, and interwoven with hope—like being held in the hand of God.

It was even suggested, that one might remember something of these ideas in the after-death realms, even though one has not been deeply experienced in a given tradition during one's lifetime.

What emerges, in overview, is that death is one step in a highly ordered ongoing process where one learns about oneself against the background tapestry of the light and the dark. It is a subjective journey through many subtle levels and realms. There are places where one can get stuck and haunted by shadows, but there are guides and teachers. The traditions suggest that the journey after death will reflect how much one has learned about this during one's lifetime.

As the level of spiritual maturity is a basic issue, all five perspectives speak of developing a relationship with our inner, eternal Essence while still in our physical body. They offer ways for us to see and work through the multiple challenges we face here. They all suggest that reflection and meditation will help us connect, before death, to the profound field of awareness that underlies and supports our consciousness. They trace our inherent longing for the light that draws us to completion.

There is a path to our evolution. It is marked by certain major transitions. Death is just one of those; there are others. The key appears to be in the wisdom and the willingness to let go when the time to do so has come.

As one accepts the journey, knowing that despite all preparation it is still a mystery, it is natural to turn one's attention to the present. Suddenly, one sees the glistening of the raindrop on the pine needle and the way the sunlight makes patterns on the wall. Questions arise: What is the quality of my "present"? What are the most valuable ways to "spend time"? And most of all, the wish raised by the Persian mystic Hafez:

One thing I hope never to regret
As I lie on my death-bed,
That I did not kiss you enough.

Epilogue

 Picture the Cosmos, the great sweep of the star-studded firmament. Picture it glowing and expanding with thousands of points of light.

Picture there, the Cosmic Christ, just in outline, with billowing cloak of brilliant blue and arms spread wide in welcome.

Hear the clear message "Remember this, at the last moment of your life."

The vision had come just before dawn. A dozen of us had been meditating throughout the night in the King's Chamber of the Great Pyramid of Giza. Each, in turn, had lain in the ancient sarcophagus, while prayers were given. I was leaning against one of the polished chamber walls. The half-remembered lines from that dream of so many years before, floated back:

"Beneath the wide and starry sky
Lay me down and let me die...

Home is the sailor, home from the sea
And the hunter home from the hills."

Christ was no longer in my back yard, frustrated. Now there was a new relationship and a deeper understanding. All journeys finish. It's natural. Whether one is "sailor" or "hunter," the arc completes. When the great adventure is over, one goes home—with faith.

BIBLIOGRAPHY

Chapter 1

Memories, Dreams and Reflections by Carl Jung, Vintage Press, Random House, 1961.

The Collected Works: The Soul and Death, Vol. 8;
The Collected Works by Carl Jung, The Bollingen Foundation, 1960.

Dreams of Death by Marie Louise von Franz, Shambhala Press, Boston & London, 1986.

Row of Tombs: Jung and Reincarnation by Sabine Lucas, 2014.

Chapter 2

Beyond the Brain: Birth, Death and Transcendence by Stanislav Grof, State University of New York Press, Albany, NY., 1985.

When the Impossible Happens: Adventures in Non-Ordinary Reality by Stanislav Grof, Sounds True, Boulder, CO., 2006.

The Ultimate Journey: Consciousness and the Mystery of Death by Stanislav Grof, Multidisciplinary Association for Psychedelic Studies, 2006.

Beyond Death, The Gates of Consciousness (Art and the Imagination) by Stanislav Grof, Thames & Hudson, New York, 1980.

Chapter 3

Autobiography of a Yogi by Paramahansa Yogananda, Self-Realization Fellowship, Los Angeles,1946.

The Second Coming of Christ: The Resurrection of the Christ Within You, Vol. and Vol. II by Paramahansa Yogananda, Self–Realization Fellowship, 2004.

Life After Death: The Burden of Proof by Deepak Chopra, Three Rivers Press, New York, 2006.

Chapter 4

The Tibetan Book of Living and Dying by Sogyal Rinpoche, HarperSanFrancisco, New York, 1994.

Mind Beyond Death by Dzogchen Ponlop, Snow Lion-Shambhala Publ., 2006.

Preparing To Die: Practical Advice and Spiritual Wisdom from the Tibetan Buddhist Tradition by Andrew Holcheck, Snow Lion-Shambhala Publ., Boston & London, 2013.

The Untethered Soul by Michael Singer, New Harbinger, Oakland, CA., 2001.

Chapter 5

Zen: Merging of East and West by Philip Kapleau, Anchor Books, New York, 1980.

Chapter 6

Esoteric Healing by Alice Bailey, Lucis Trust, New York, 1953.

A Treatise on Cosmic Fire by Alice Bailey, Lucis Trust, New York, 1972.

Externalization of the Hierarchy by Alice Bailey, Lucis Trust, New York, 1957.

Chapter 7

Being Mortal: Medicine and What Matters in the End by Atul Gawande, Penguin, 2014.

BERNICE H. HILL, PH.D.

Bernice H. Hill, Ph.D. is a Jungian analyst in private practice in Boulder, Colorado for over thirty years. She is a member of the International Association for Analytic Psychology (Zurich) and a senior training analyst with the C. G. Jung Institute of Colorado. She is a certified facilitator of the Stanislav and Christina Grofs' Holotropic Breathwork™ and has written this book for her children, her grandchildren and all other explorers of Spirit.